Road Race

Follow the maze to the Finish Line.

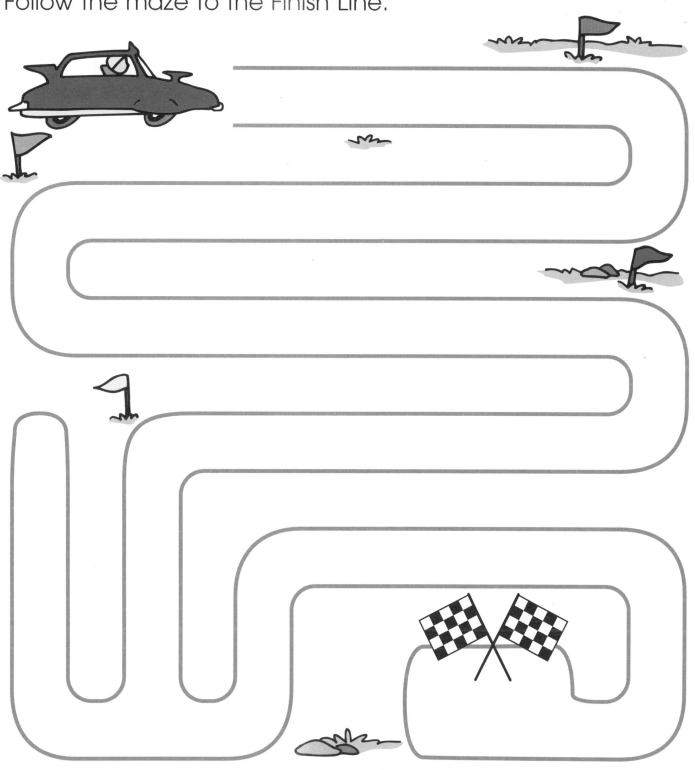

1

Tunnel

Help the prairie dog find its way home.
Draw the path.

Where's My Cave?

Help the dragon find its cave.
Draw the path.

Cave

Under the Sea

Help the starfish find its starfish family.
Draw the path.

All Kinds of Leaves

Trace each leaf.

Animal Shapes

Trace each animal.

Draw What's Missing

Draw the missing parts.

Finish the Pictures

Finish each picture to match.

Pumpkin Patch

Draw lines between the matching pumpkins.

All Kinds of Vegetables

Draw lines between the matching vegetables.

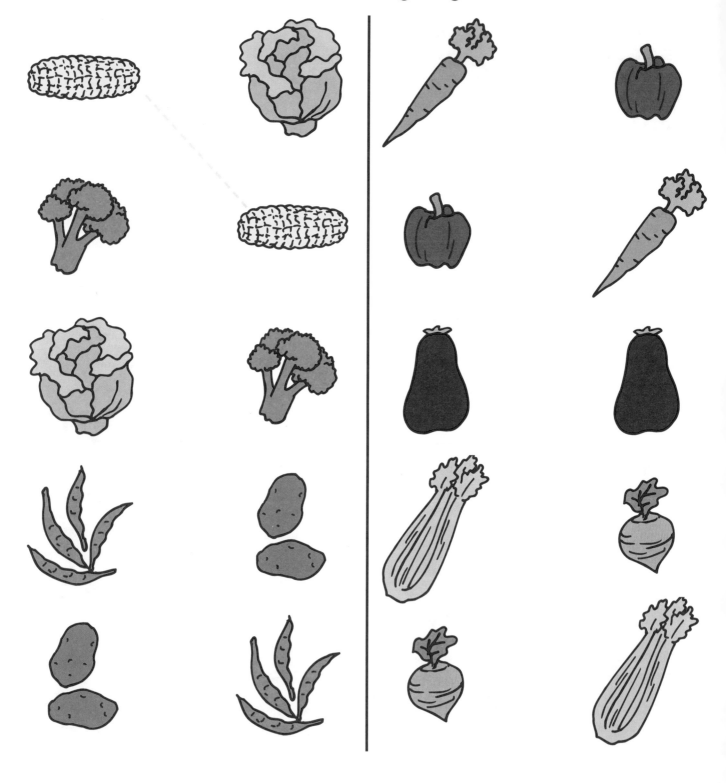

Shadow Fun

Match each picture to its shadow.

Truck Shadows

Match each truck to its shadow.

Writing Uppercase Letters

Color, trace, and write each letter.

A   __ __

B   __ __

C   __ __

D   __ __

E   __ __

F   __ __

G   __ __

H   __ __

I   __ __

J   __ __

K   __ __

L   __ __

M   __ __

N   __ __

More Uppercase Letters

Color, trace, and write each letter.

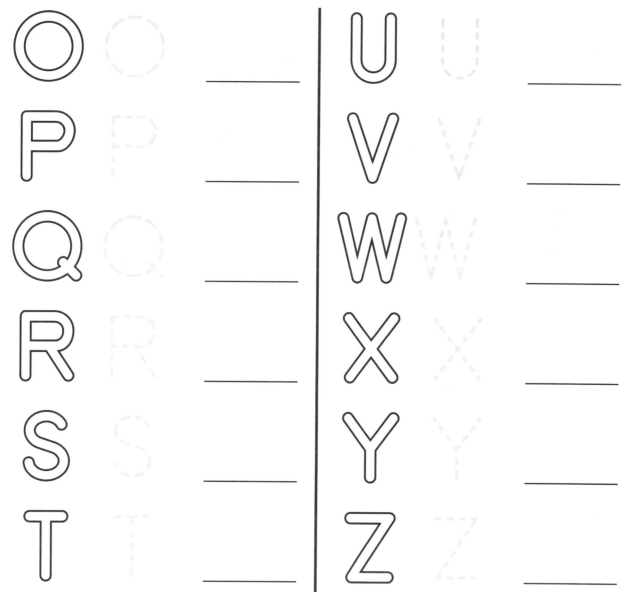

O   _____   U   _____

P   _____   V   _____

Q   _____   W   _____

R   _____   X   _____

S   _____   Y   _____

T   _____   Z   _____

Writing Lowercase Letters

Color, trace, and write each letter.

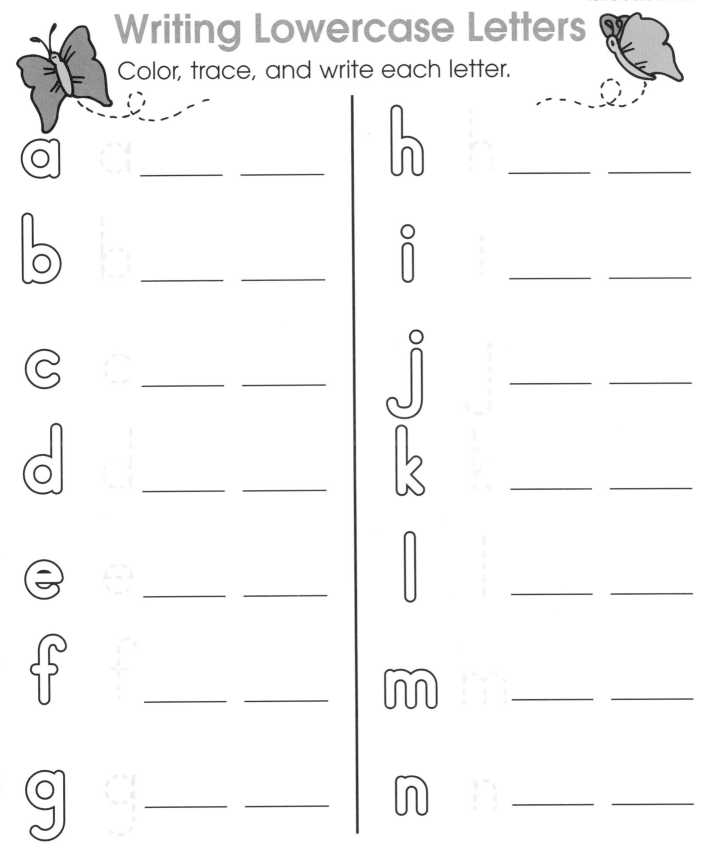

a

b

c

d

e

f

g

h

i

j

k

l

m

n

More Lowercase Letters

Color, trace, and write each letter.

o ___ ___ ___   u ___ ___ ___

p ___ ___ ___   v ___ ___ ___

q ___ ___ ___   w ___ ___ ___

r ___ ___ ___   x ___ ___ ___

s ___ ___ ___   y ___ ___ ___

t ___ ___ ___   z ___ ___ ___

In the Woods

Connect the dots from **A** to **Z**.

At the Park

Connect the dots from **A** to **Z**.

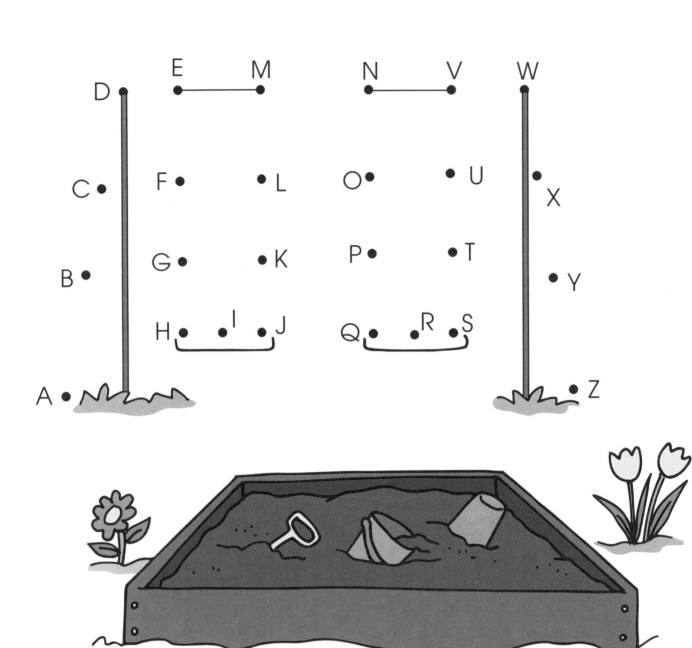

What Is It?

Connect the dots from **a** to **z**.

Sailing, Sailing

Connect the dots from **a** to **z**.

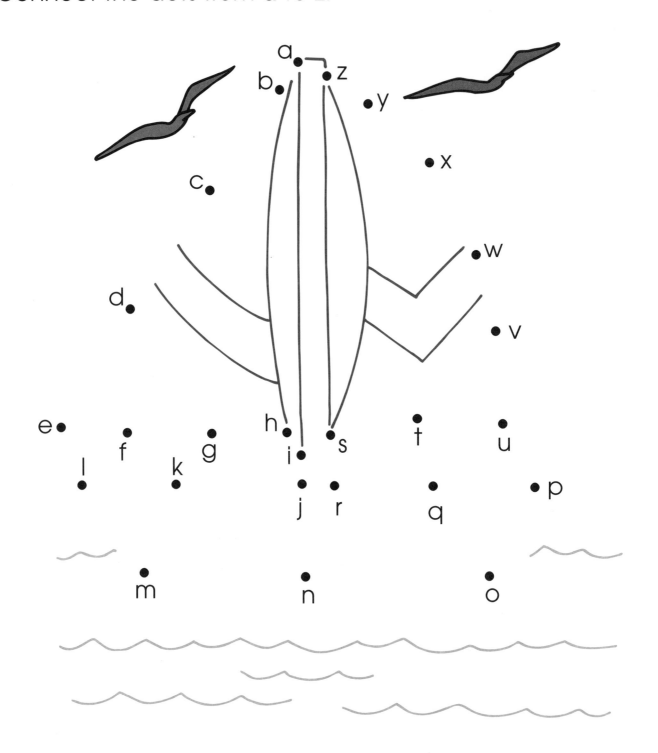

Alphabet Match-up
Draw lines to match the letters.

a	C	n	K	s	U
b	A	k	L	t	V
c	D	l	J	u	S
d	B	m	N	v	W
e	F	j	P	w	T
f	E	o	M	x	Z
g	I	p	O	y	X
h	H	q	R	z	Y
i	G	r	Q		

A Bunch of Balloons

Draw lines to match the letters.

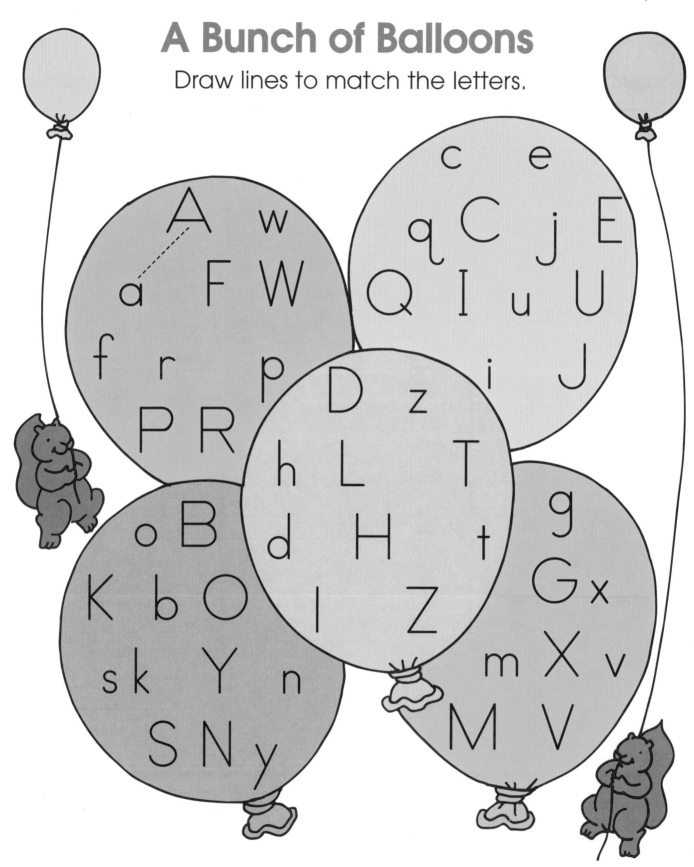

 # Alphabet Practice

Read the letters. Write the letters.

Aa   Bb

Cc   Dd

Ee   Ff

Gg   Hh

Ii   Jj

Kk   Ll

Mm   Nn

More Alphabet Practice

Read the letters. Write the letters.

Oo

Pp

Qq

Rr

Ss

Tt

Uu

Vv

Ww

Xx

Yy

Zz

Alphabet Fun

Write the missing lowercase letters in the big box.
Then trace over all the letters with a crayon.

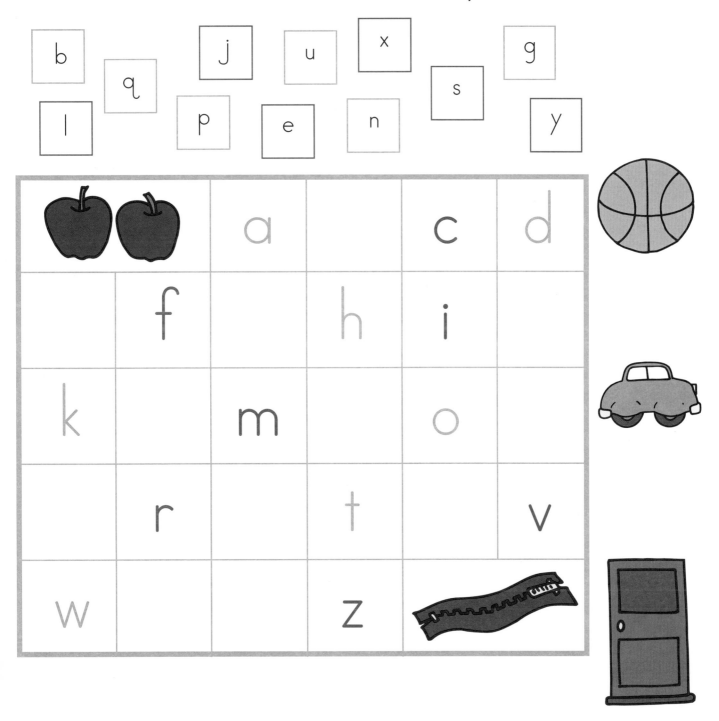

b   j   u   x   g

q

l   p   e   n   s   y

	a		c	d
f		h	i	
k	m		o	
r		t		v
w		z		

Alphabet Critter

Write the letters from **A** to **Z**.

What a Worm!

Write the letters from **a** to **z**.

Missing Letters

Write the missing letters.

A a B b c D

E f G h

i J k L

m N O p

Q r s T

U v W x

y Z

Aa to Zz

Write the missing letters.

Matching Sounds

Draw lines between the pictures that begin with the same sound.

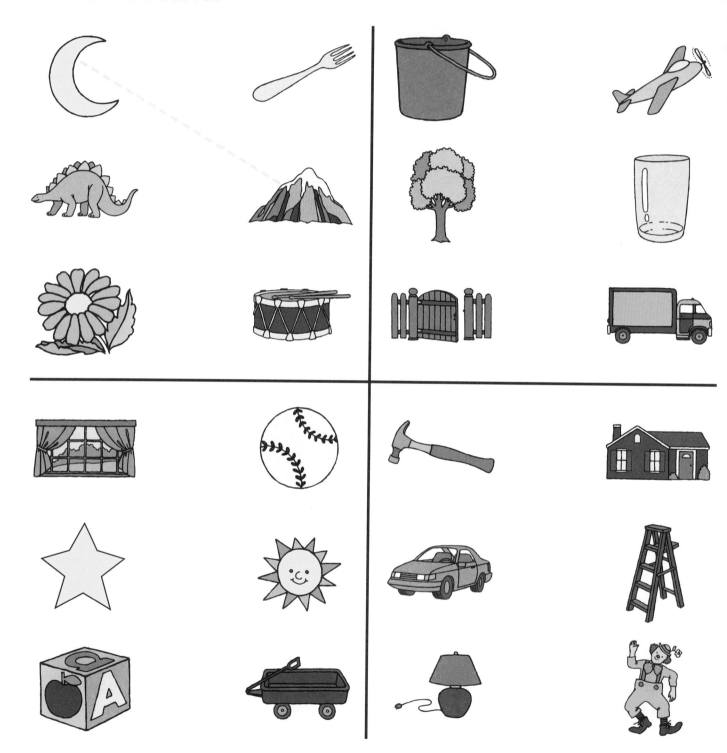

30

Match-up

Draw lines between the pictures that begin with the same sound.

Ball, Book, and Butterfly

Circle the pictures that start with the sound shown.
Draw an **X** on the picture that doesn't match.

Turtle, Top, and Ten

Circle the pictures that start with the sound shown.
Draw an **X** on the picture that doesn't match.

What Sound Does It Start With?

Look at the picture. What sound does it start with?
Circle the matching letter.

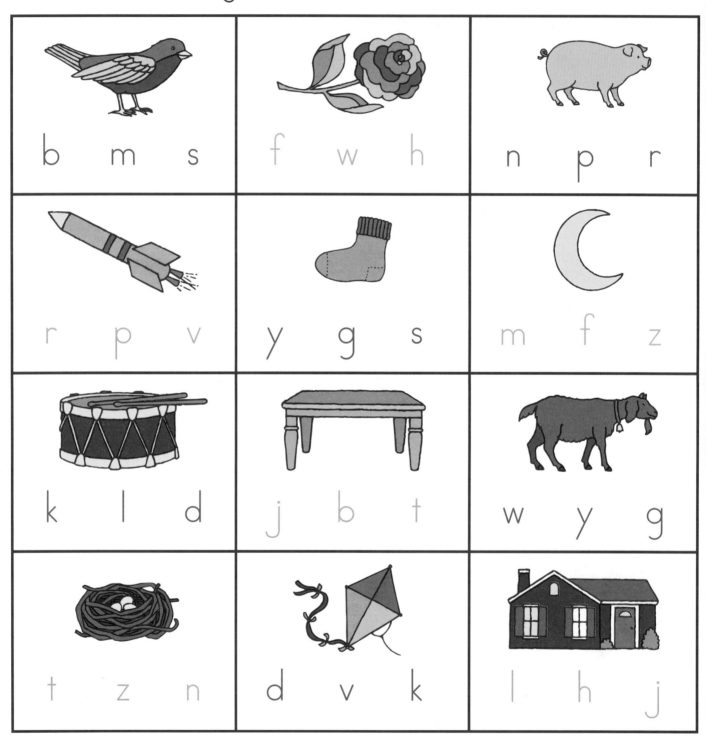

b   m   s   f   w   h   n   p   r

r   p   v   y   g   s   m   f   z

k   l   d   j   b   t   w   y   g

t   z   n   d   v   k   l   h   j

What's the Sound?

Look at the picture. What sound does it start with?
Circle the matching letter.

p m t	p f b	d k b
c r l	r f n	t l x
d m n	z r s	r m d
g t l	h k p	r z j

35

What's the Letter?

Look at the pictures. Write the beginning sound.

What Comes First?

Look at the pictures. Write the beginning sound.

Make a Match

Draw lines to match the pictures to the sounds.

Making Pictures

Draw pictures that begin with the sounds.

b	v
z	p
r	l
t	f

Colors

Trace and write.

red

_____

- - - - - - - - - - - - - - - - - -

_____

blue

_____

- - - - - - - - - - - - - - - - - -

_____

black

_____

- - - - - - - - - - - - - - - - - -

_____

orange

_____

- - - - - - - - - - - - - - - - - -

_____

More Colors

Trace and write.

green

_____

- - - - - - - - - - - - - - - - - - - -

_____

brown

_____

- - - - - - - - - - - - - - - - - - - -

_____

purple

_____

- - - - - - - - - - - - - - - - - - - -

_____

yellow

_____

- - - - - - - - - - - - - - - - - - - -

_____

Monster Colors

Trace and color.

green

black

yellow

orange

purple

blue

brown

red

The Rain Forest

Color.

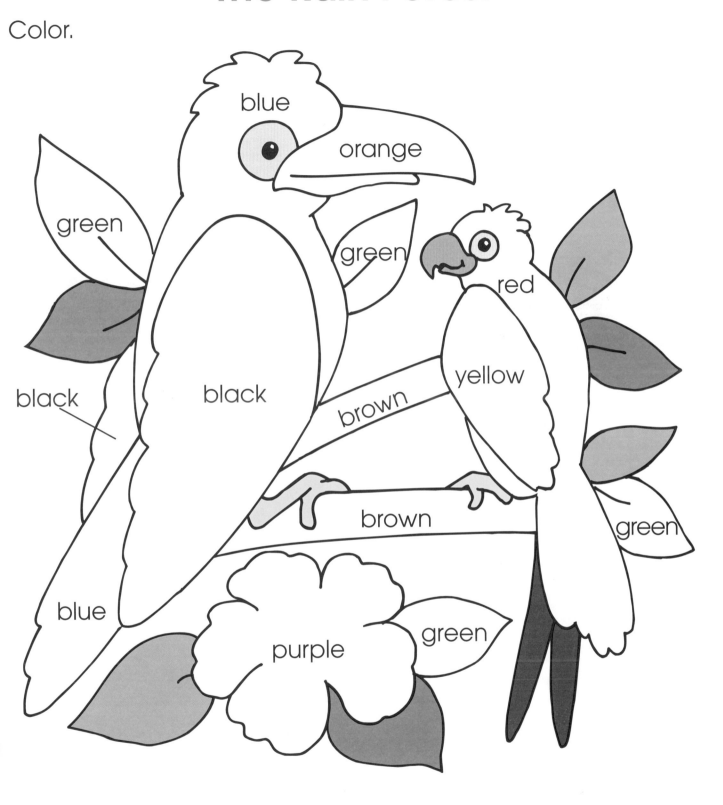

What Color Is It?

Match.

purple

red

blue

green

black

yellow

brown

orange

Many Colors

Draw a line from each color word to the matching picture.
Draw an **X** on the color word that doesn't belong.

leaves	green	brown	purple
apples	red	yellow	black
cats	orange	green	black
grapes	orange	purple	green
water	red	green	blue

45

Circles

Trace.   Draw.

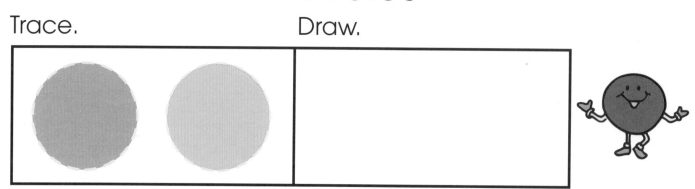

Color only the circles.

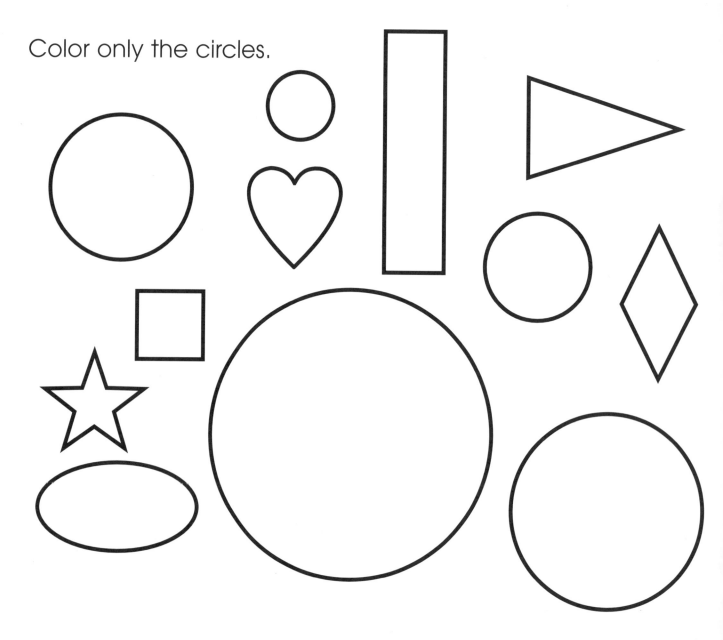

Squares

Trace.   Draw.

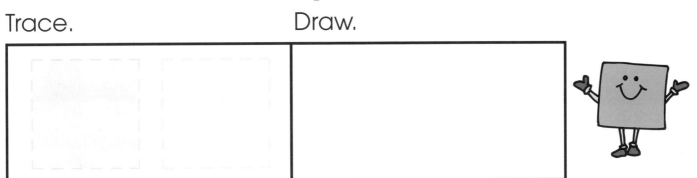

Color only the squares.

Triangles

Trace. | Draw.

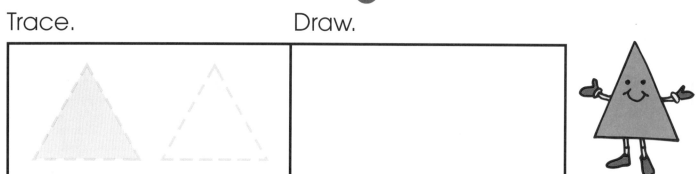

Color only the triangles.

Rectangles

Trace.   Draw.

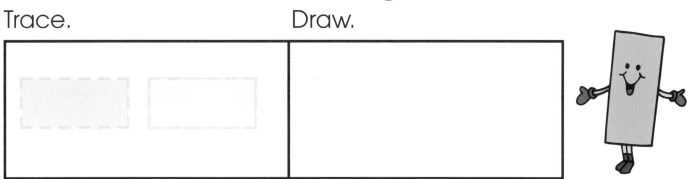

Color only the rectangles.

Lots of Shapes

Trace.	Draw.
oval	
diamond	
heart	
star	

Shapes

Trace. Color.

Home Sweet Home

Color:

◯ yellow   ▭ green   ▲ red   ◼ blue

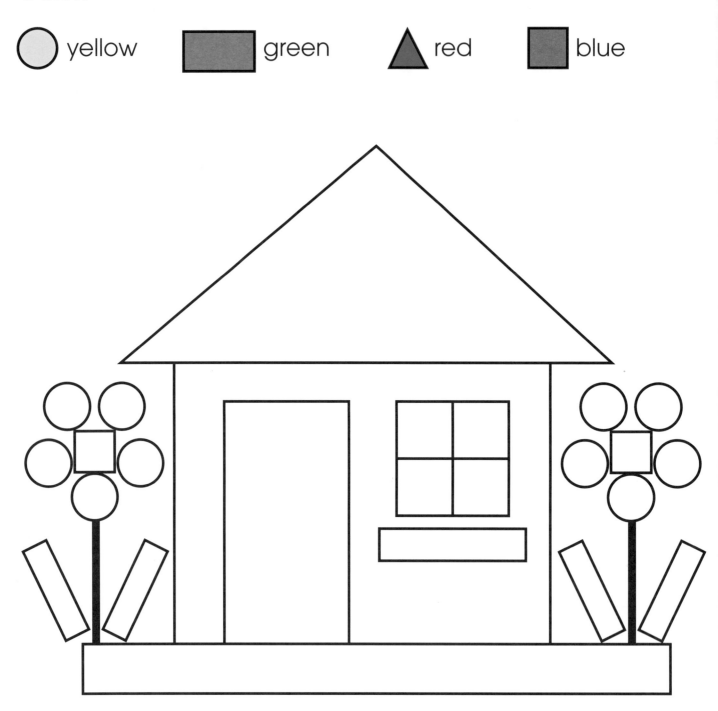

Spring Flowers

Color:

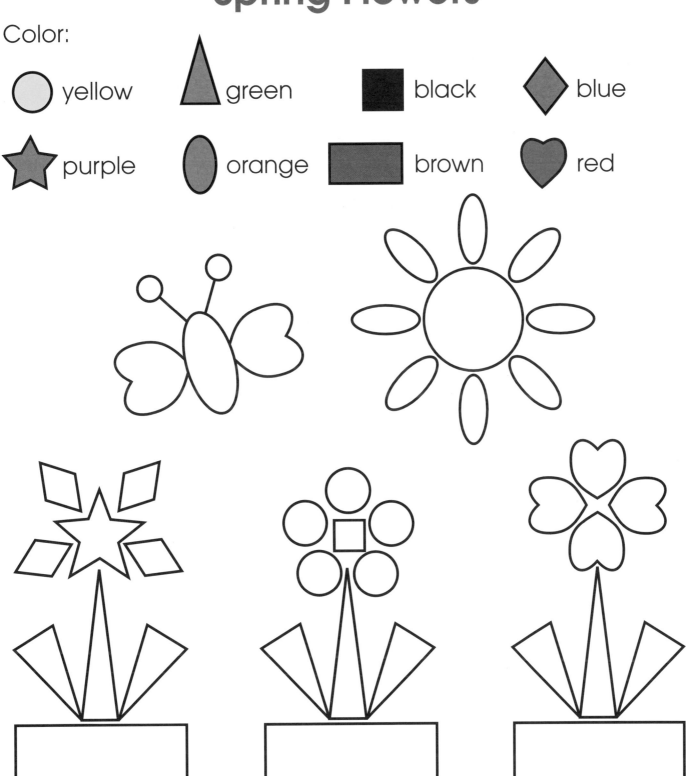

A Tile Design

Color:

- ⬤ yellow
- ▭ green
- ◆ black
- ▲ blue
- ♥ purple
- ⬭ orange
- ■ brown
- ★ red

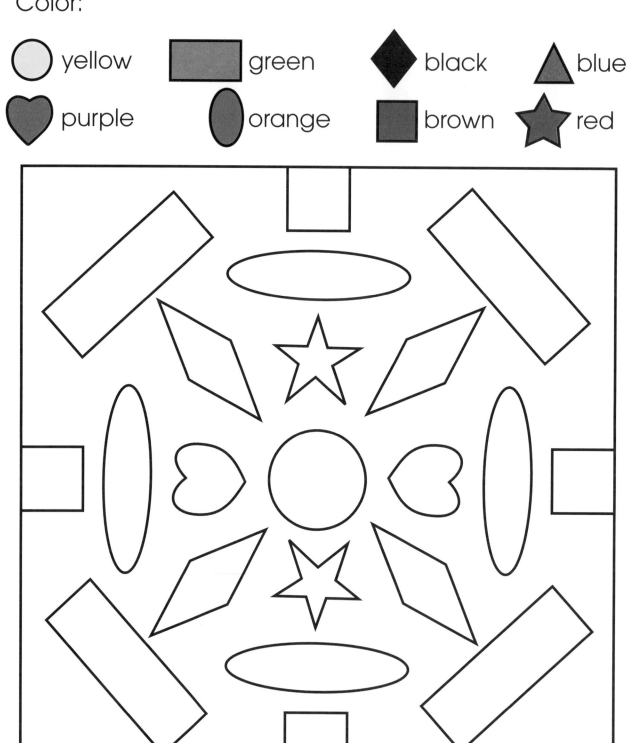

Color Patterns

Color. Finish the pattern.

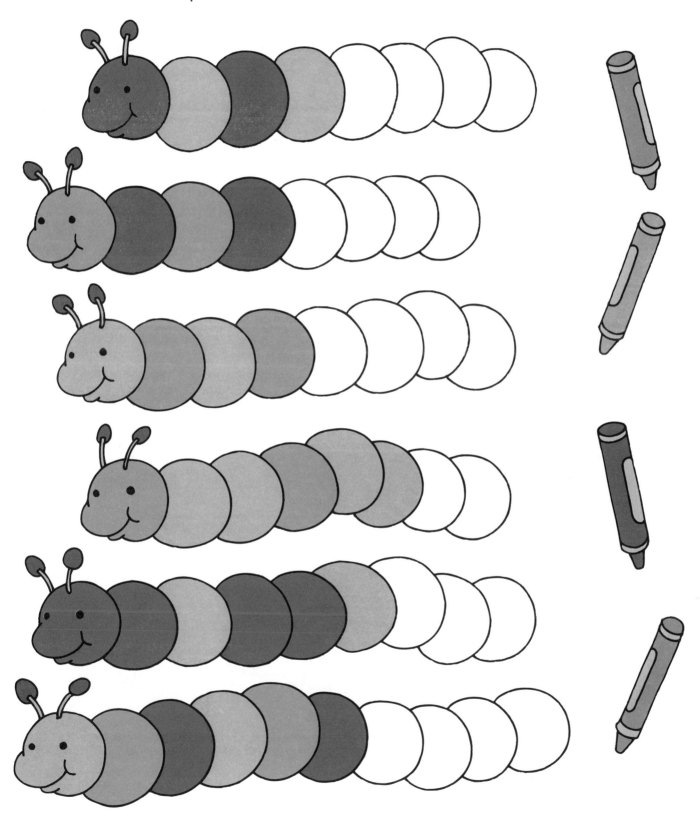

Pattern People

Color. Finish the pattern.

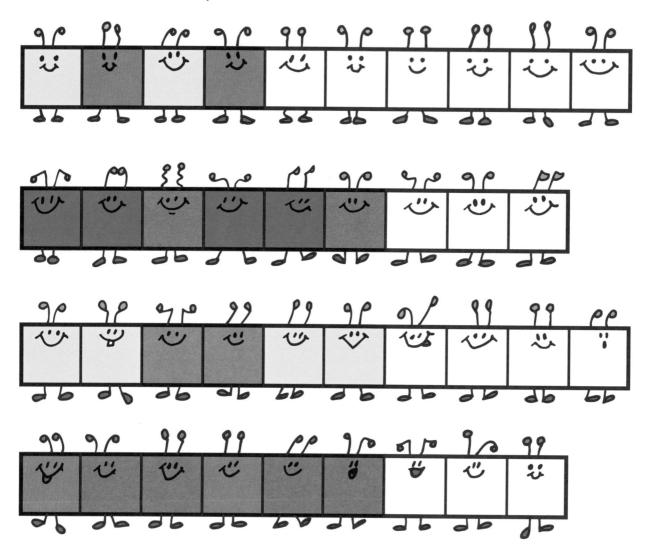

Use two colors to make your own pattern.

Shape Patterns

Say the pattern aloud. Draw the missing shapes.

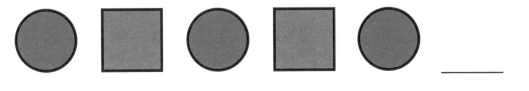

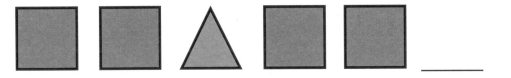

Choose two shapes. Draw your own pattern.

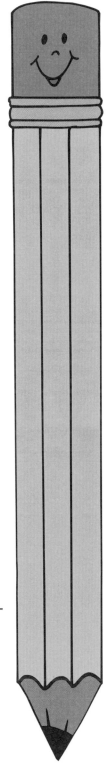

What Shape Comes Next?

Say the pattern aloud. Draw the missing shapes.

Draw your own shape pattern.

Writing Numbers 1 to 5
Count. Trace. Write.

•   1   1

• •   2   2

• • •   3   3

• • • •   4   4

• • • • •   5   5

 # Writing Numbers 6 to 10
Count. Trace. Write.

6   6

7   7

8   8

9   9

10   10

Writing 1 to 10

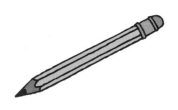

Color, trace, and write each number.

1	6
2	7
3	8
4	9
5	10

Desert Life

Circle **2**.

Circle **4**.

Circle **I**.

Circle **3**.

Circle **5**.

Circle **6**.

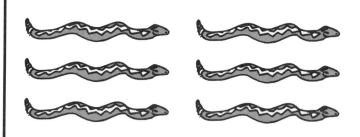

Circle **8**.

Circle **7**.

Out in Space

Count. Write the number.

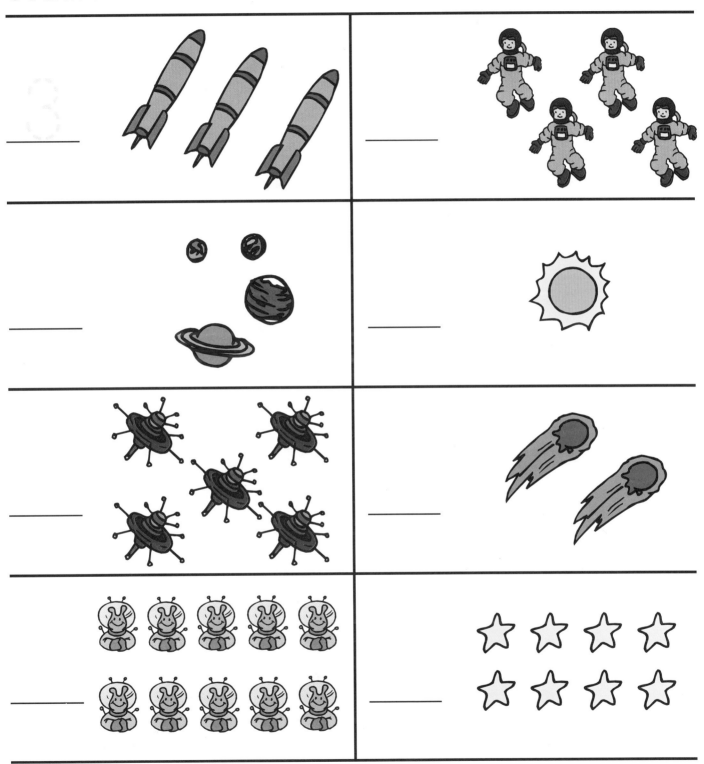

Hats Off!

Count. Write the number.

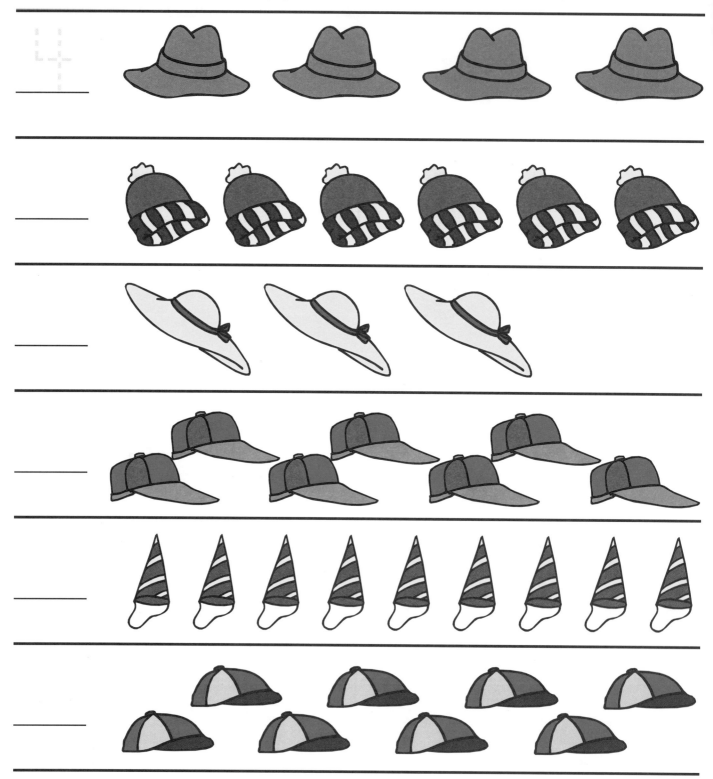

A Writing Tool

Connect the dots from **1** to **10**.

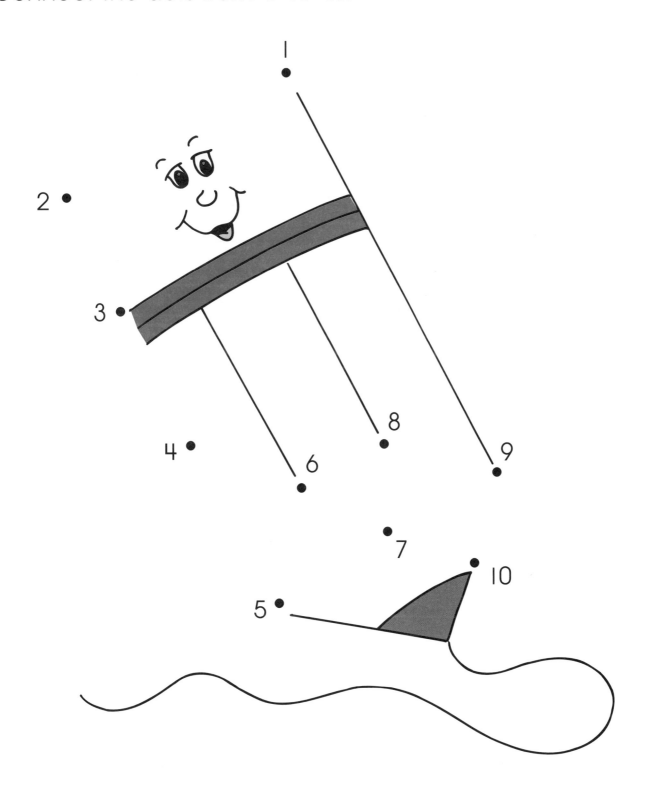

Number Boxes

Trace.

1	2	3	4	5
6	7	8	9	10
11	12	13	14	15
16	17	18	19	20

Write.

1				

Happy Numbers

Write the numbers from 1 to 20.

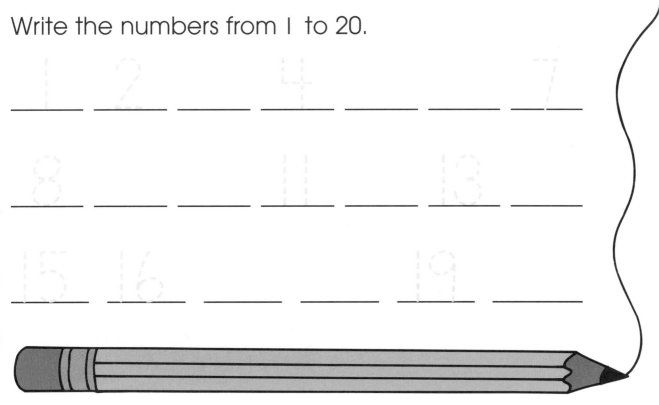

A Long Time Ago

Connect the dots from **1** to **20**.

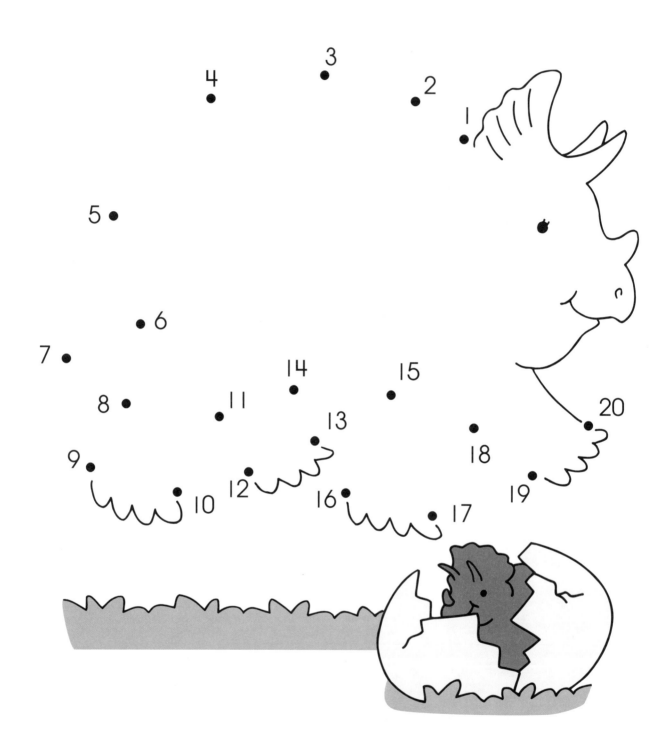

Number Patterns
Write the missing numbers.

1, 2, ___, 4, ___, 6, 7, ___, 9, 10

8, ___, 10, 11, ___, 13, 14, ___

10, 11, ___, 13, ___, 15, ___, 17

14, ___, 16, ___, 18, ___, 20

3, ___, 5, 6, 7, ___, 9, ___, ___

2, ___, 4, ___, 6, ___, 8, ___, 10

Missing Numbers
Write the missing numbers.

0, 1, 2, ___, 4, ___, 6, ___, 8, 9

8, 9, ___, 11, 12, ___, 14, ___

12, 13, ___, ___, 16, 17, ___, 19

13, 14, ___, 16, ___, 18, ___, 20

___, 1, 2, ___, 4, ___, 6, 7, ___

1, ___, 3, ___, 5, ___, 7, ___, 9

Add Them Up

Count. Write. Add.

2 + 3 = ____
____   ____   ____

____ + ____ = ____

____ + ____ = ____

____ + ____ = ____

____ + ____ = ____

____ + ____ = ____

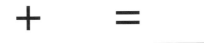 

____ + ____ = ____

____ + ____ = ____

Sports Fun

Add. Write the math sentence.

$\underline{1} + \underline{3} = \underline{4}$

$\underline{} + \underline{} = \underline{}$

$\underline{} + \underline{} = \underline{}$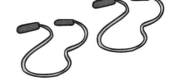

$\underline{} + \underline{} = \underline{}$

$\underline{} + \underline{} = \underline{}$

$\underline{} + \underline{} = \underline{}$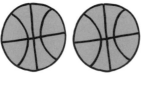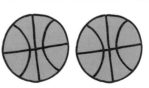

$\underline{} + \underline{} = \underline{}$

Buttons

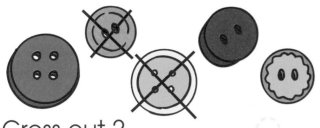

Cross out 2.
How many are left?

Cross out 1.
How many are left?

Cross out 3.
How many are left?

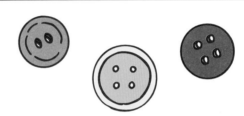

Cross out 0.
How many are left?

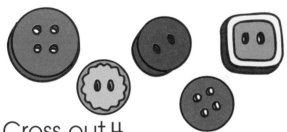

Cross out 4.
How many are left?

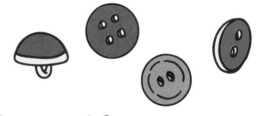

Cross out 2.
How many are left?

Cross out 3.
How many are left?

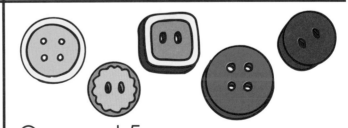

Cross out 5.
How many are left?

Dinosaurs

Cross out 4. How many are left?

2

Cross out 3. How many are left?

_____

Cross out 0. How many are left?

_____

Cross out 2. How many are left?

_____

Cross out 1. How many are left?

_____

What a Day!

What did you like doing at school today?
Draw a picture of it. Finish the sentence.

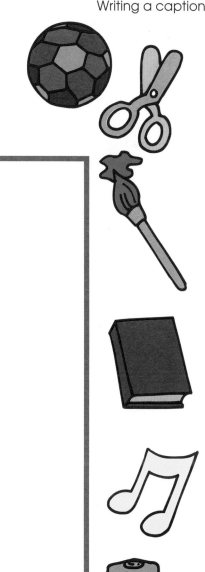

At school today I liked

What a Place!

Think of a real or make-believe place.
Draw a picture of it.
Write a sentence about it.

A Very Important Person

Draw a picture of someone important to you.

Write a sentence about him or her.

The Day the Monster Came

A silly monster has come to school.
Draw a picture of it.
Write a question you would like to ask it.

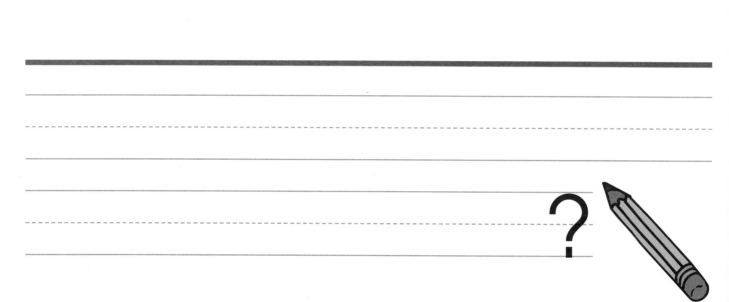

A Thank-you Note

Draw a picture showing how someone helped you.
Write **Thank you!** below it.

Learning to Spell

Have someone help you make a list of words you want to learn to spell.

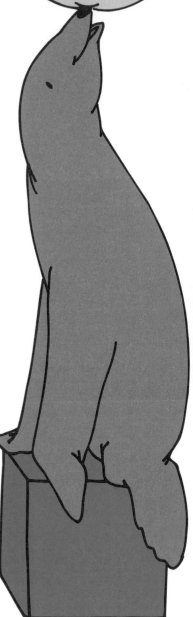

Read the word. Spell it aloud. Trace it. Write it.

My Favorite Part

Listen to a story. What story did you listen to?

Draw your favorite part.

The Best Part

Listen to a storybook. Draw your favorite part of the book.

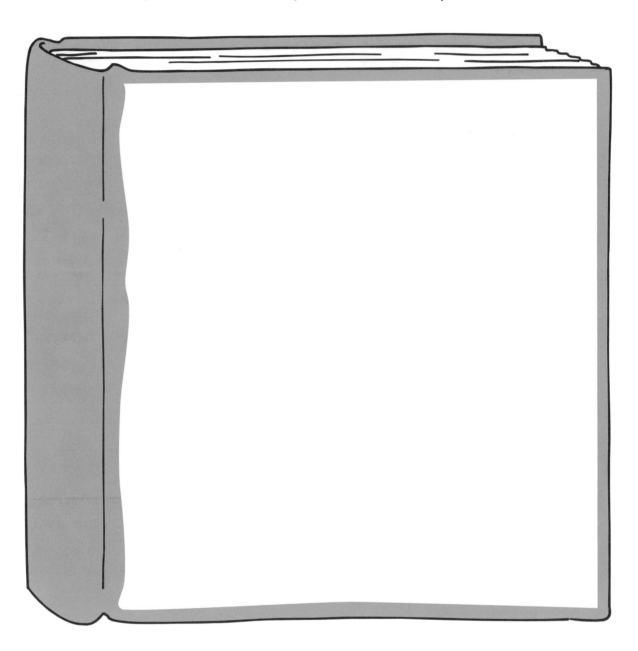

The part I liked best was

That Doesn't Belong!

Circle the pictures that belong in the group.
Draw an **X** on the picture that doesn't belong.

83

Sorry, Wrong Group

Circle the pictures that belong in the group.
Draw an **X** on the picture that doesn't belong.

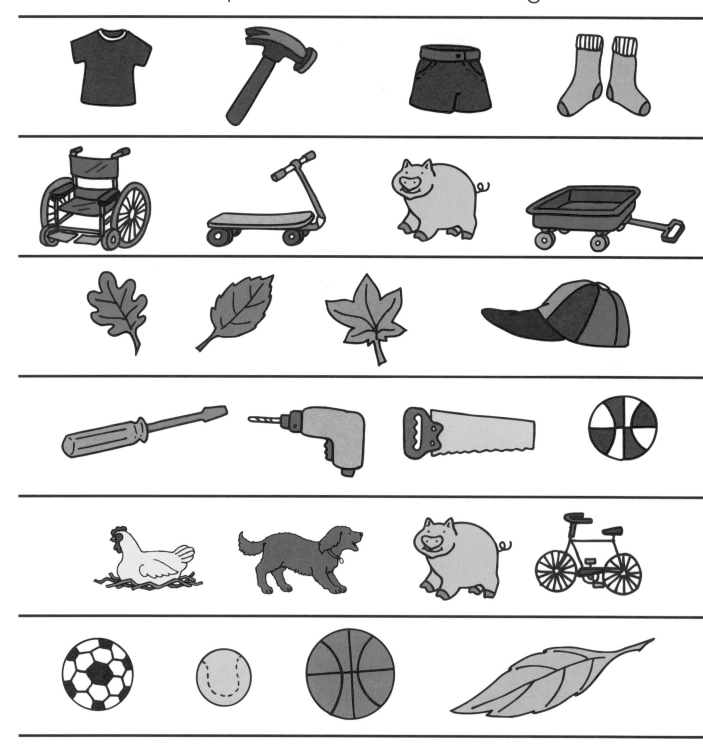

What Happens Next?

Look at the picture. Draw a line to the box that shows what happens next.

Dinosaur Friends

Look at the picture. Draw a line to the box that shows what happens next.

Does It Belong?

Circle the five things in the picture that do not belong.

Kindergarten

What do you like best about kindergarten?
Draw a picture. Finish the sentence.

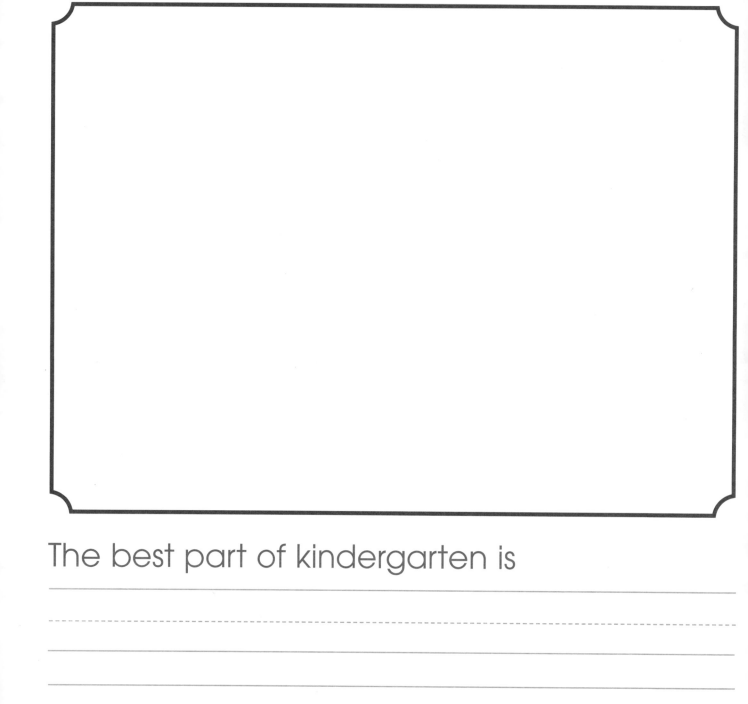

The best part of kindergarten is

Someone Special

Finish the sentences.
Draw what you would like to do for your birthday.

My name is

_____

- - - - - - - - - - - - - - - - - -

_____

My birthday is

_____

- - - - - - - - - - - - - - - - - -

_____

Meet My Family

Finish the sentence. Draw a picture of your family.

There are _____ people in my family.
Here we are!

My Family

Finish the sentence. Draw a picture of your family.

My family is important to me because

Where I Live

Draw your home. Write your address.

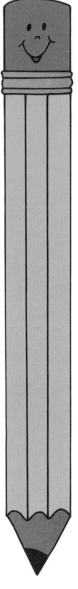

My address is

92

Home Safety

My name is

My address is

If I need help, I can call

My Phone Number

Write your phone number.

My phone number is

_____

- -

_____

Telephone Talk

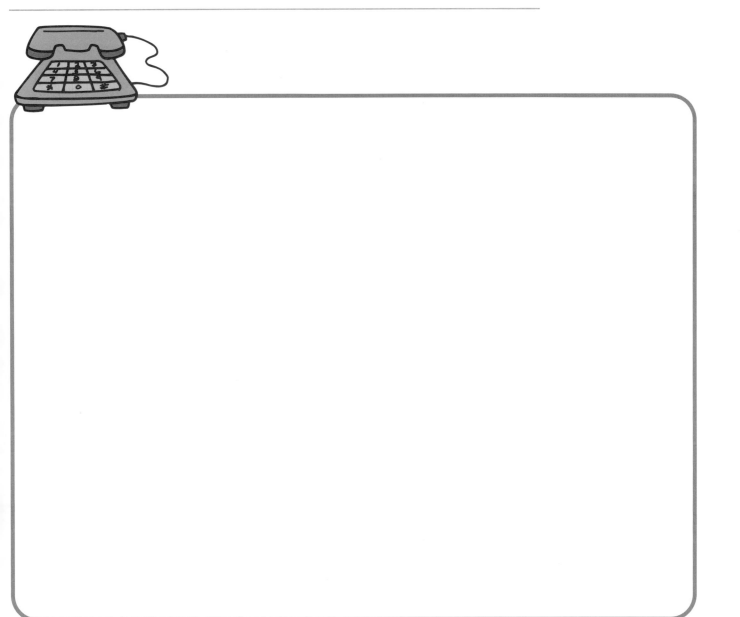

Write your phone number.
Draw yourself talking politely on the telephone.

My phone number is

_____

- -

_____

Super Kid Award

Color Super Kid to look like you. Finish the sentence.

I am a Super Kid because I

_____

- -

_____